FOREWORD

Book 3 of this Method is quite a milestone for a young pupil to reach, as he or she is introduced to third position and new major and minor keys, in addition to fourth finger extensions and half position.

The third position work is slow and thorough so there are numerous exercises, along with plenty of tuneful solos and duets which can be played at the same time. These should keep interest alive while technical difficulties are surmounted.

The bowing exercises at the beginning give ample opportunity for the pupil to study all types of bowing:

    Whole bows and half bows at heel and point
    Short bows at heel, point and middle
    Martelé
    Spiccato
    Sautillé

These studies are short and simple and easily memorised so that full attention can be given to the right arm. They should be studied concurrently with the contents of the book – one or two with each step.

If bowing technique is well established, the pupil will have the necessary confidence to tackle the more advanced work in Book 4. Then the pupil will have to play pieces with much more varied types of bowing. He/she will also study second, fourth and fifth positions, trills, double stopping, and so on.

I hope that children will enjoy these pieces. I played many of them in my youth and would like to see them kept alive.

ETA COHEN

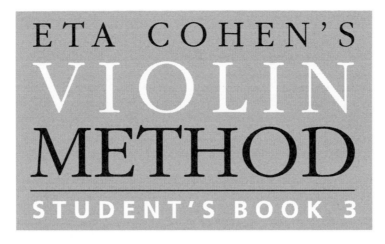

ETA COHEN'S VIOLIN METHOD

STUDENT'S BOOK 3

Teacher's accompaniment book available separately

Novello Publishing Limited

Exclusive distributors:
Hal Leonard
7777 West Bluemound Road, Milwaukee, WI 53213
Email: info@halleonard.com
Hal Leonard Europe Limited
42 Wigmore Street Maryleborne, London, WIU 2 RN
Email: info@halleonardeurope.com
Hal Leonard Australia Pty. Ltd.
4 Lentara Court Cheltenham, Victoria, 9132 Australia
Email: info@halleonard.com.au

Order No. NOV916172   ISBN 0-85360-184-4

Cover design by xheight design Limited

CONTENTS OF PIECES

Bowing Exercises

	Study in C *2*
	Study in Whole Bows *3*
	Study in G *3*
	Study in Crossing Strings *3*
Step 1	Minuet in A Minor *4*
	Bohemian Polka *4*
Step 2	Three Hebrew Folk Tunes *5*
Step 3	Minuet *6*
Step 4	Song of Hope *7*
	Hebrew Folk Tune – Kinneret *7*
	Greensleeves *7*
Step 5	The Ash Grove *8*
	Adagio *8*
	Ayre *8*
Step 6	The River *9*
	French Melody *9*
	Country Dance *9*
Step 7	Valsette *10*
Step 8	The Shepherdess *12*
Step 9	Hot Cross Buns *13*
	Will Ye No Come Back Again *13*
Step 10	Swanee River *14*
	The Harp That Once *14*
	For He's a Jolly Good Fellow *14*
	Sing a Song of Sixpence *14*
	John Peel *14*
Step 11	All Through the Night *15*
	Men of Harlech *15*
	Polly Put the Kettle On *15*
Step 12	Yankee Doodle *16*
	Polish Folk Tune *16*
	St Paul's Steeple *16*

	Lavender's Blue *16*
Step 13	Peasants' Dance *17*
	Allegro (La Rejouissance) *17*
Step 14	Study in First and Third Positions *18*
	Song of Freedom *18*
Step 15	Concerto in D Minor for Two Violins *19*
Step 16	Serenade *20*
	March *20*
Step 17	Study *21*
Step 18	Study *22*
	Gaelic Song *22*
	Meeting of the Waters *22*
Step 19	Study *23*
	Gentle Maiden *23*
	Valse Sentimentale *23*
Step 20	Study in First and Third Positions *24*
	A Little Piece *24*
Step 21	Allegretto *25*
	Largo *25*
Step 22	Menuett *26*
Step 23	Minuet in G *27*
	Londonderry Air *27*
Step 24	Ave Maria *28*
	The Last Rose of Summer *28*
Step 25	Gavotte in D *29*
Step 26	Ave Maria *30*
Step 27	Minuet *31*
Step 28	Entr'acte *32*
	La Serenata *32*
Step 29	Preludio *33*
	Allemanda *33*
	Sarabanda *33*
Step 30	Preludio *34*
	Tempo di Gavotta *34*

ETA COHEN VIOLIN METHOD
Book 3
BOWING EXERCISES

These exercises are intended as an indication of the lines on which the right arm should be developed, but the teacher can improvise many more with varying dynamics. One or two bowing exercises should be practised every week.

SCALES

Practise all scales with the types of bowing indicated. The examples will only be shown in the scale of G major.

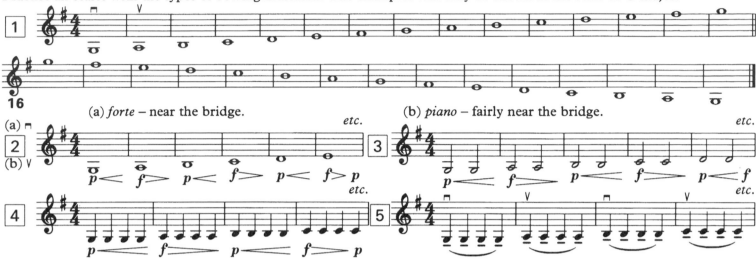

(a) *forte* – near the bridge. (b) *piano* – fairly near the bridge.

STUDY IN C

Practise first with half bows a) middle to point, b) heel to middle, then as follows:

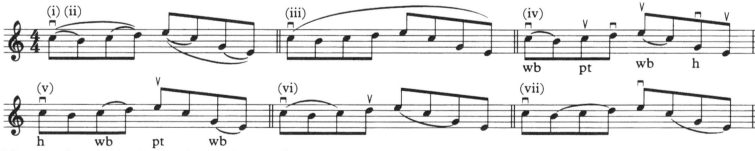

Nos. 4 and 5 can also be practised with martelé bowing.

Detaché at moderate speed;
(a) at the point of the bow,
(b) in the middle of the bow, } *forte and piano*
(c) at the heel of the bow.

Detaché at quick speed;
(a) at the point of the bow,
(b) in the middle of the bow. } *forte and piano*

Variations (viii) and (ix) could also be practised with spiccato and sautillé bowing, both forte and piano.

STUDY IN WHOLE BOWS
(Whole bows throughout)

STUDY IN G
(With varied bowings)

To be practised as follows:

(i)
(ii)
(iii)

(iv) detaché, spiccato and sautillé.

STUDY IN CROSSING STRINGS
(Martelé bowing)

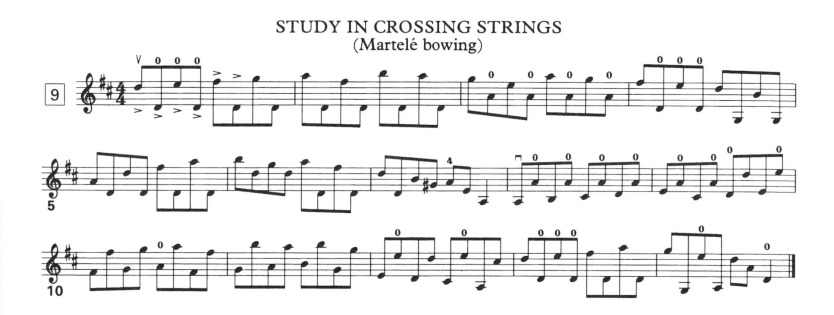

STEP 1
EXERCISES FOR THE EXTENSION OF THE 4th FINGER

MINUET IN A MINOR

HANDEL

SCALE OF C MAJOR – 2 OCTAVES
(Also practise slurred with 2 beats to a bow)

(Also practise slurred with 3 beats to a bow)

BOHEMIAN POLKA

STEP 2
SCALE OF A MINOR

THREE HEBREW FOLK TUNES
I YEARNING

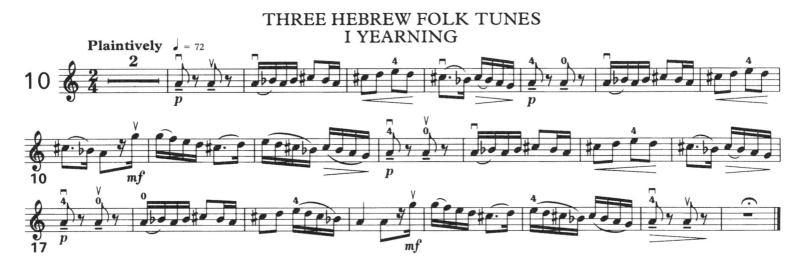

II SLOW DANCE

III HAVA NAGILA

STEP 3
SCALE OF E MINOR

EXERCISE TO SHOW THE USE OF HALF POSITION AND EXTENSIONS

MINUET

PURCELL

SCALE OF B MINOR

STEP 5

SCALE OF E MAJOR

27

THE ASH GROVE

28

ADAGIO

CORELLI

29

SCALE OF D MINOR

30

31

AYRE

PURCELL

32

STEP 6
SCALE OF G MINOR

STEP 7
VALSETTE

JOHN HENLEY

88

97

106

115

123

132

141

151

157

162

167

STEP 8
THE THIRD POSITION

The pupil should play all the following exercises (until Step 19) with the hand in the third position. No attempt should be made to move from one position to another. The octaves should all be played to check intonation but the unison double stops can be omitted if too difficult.

EXERCISES USING FIRST THREE FINGERS ONLY

Can be played also on the G and D strings.

THIRD POSITION STUDY

THE SHEPHERDESS

STEP 9
SCALES AND ARPEGGIOS IN THIRD POSITION

3rd and 4th fingers must be *very close together*.

EXERCISES IN THE THIRD POSITION

HOT CROSS BUNS

WILL YE NO COME BACK AGAIN

STEP 10
SWANEE RIVER

THE HARP THAT ONCE

FOR HE'S A JOLLY GOOD FELLOW

SING A SONG OF SIXPENCE

JOHN PEEL

* Backward extension on F♯. Hand should not move back, only finger.

STEP 11
SCALE OF C MAJOR – 2 OCTAVES

Keep the 2nd and 3rd fingers very close together on the A and E strings.

ALL THROUGH THE NIGHT

MEN OF HARLECH

POLLY PUT THE KETTLE ON

STEP 12
SCALE OF F MAJOR

Arpeggio

61

YANKEE DOODLE

Swaggeringly ♩ = 184

62

mf staccato

POLISH FOLK TUNE

With a gentle lilt ♩ = 152

63

p

cresc.

dim. pp

rit.

8

Novello & Company Ltd.

SCALE OF D MAJOR

64

SCALE OF D MINOR

65

ARPEGGIOS

Major

66

Minor

67

ST PAUL'S STEEPLE

A Chime ♩ = 138

68

f

ff

7

LAVENDER'S BLUE

Simply ♩ = 108

69

mp

mf

p

9

18

STEP 13
PEASANTS' DANCE

J.S. BACH

ALLEGRO (LA REJOUISSANCE)
(from *Fireworks Music*)

G.F. HANDEL

* Backward extension of 1st finger. Hand must stay in third position.

STEP 14
ARPEGGIOS

Exercises 72–79 include shifts only before or after open strings.

EXERCISE IN SHIFTING
(Open string shifts only)

Practise first with bowing below, then with bowing above.

STUDY IN FIRST AND THIRD POSITIONS
(Open string shifts)

SONG OF FREEDOM

STEP 15
CONCERTO IN D MINOR FOR TWO VIOLINS

VIVALDI

Forcefully
Violin I

Forcefully
Violin II

STEP 16
SERENADE

GOUNOD

MARCH
(from *Occasional Oratorio*)

HANDEL

STEP 17
EXERCISES IN GLIDING FROM FIRST TO THIRD POSITION
USING THE SAME FINGER

STUDY

WOHLFAHRT

STEP 18
EXERCISES IN GLIDING FROM FIRST TO THIRD POSITION
AND FROM THIRD TO FIRST POSITION USING THE SAME FINGER

STUDY

Adapted from study by Kayser

GAELIC SONG

from 'Graded Melodies', DORMAN

Novello & Company Ltd.

MEETING OF THE WATERS

from 'Graded Melodies', DORMAN

Novello & Company Ltd.

STEP 19
STUDY
(Shifting on the same finger)

Adapted from study by Wohlfahrt

GENTLE MAIDEN

IRISH
arr. Henry Tolhurst

VALSE SENTIMENTALE

SCHUBERT

STEP 20
EXERCISES IN GLIDING FROM ONE FINGER TO ANOTHER
BY MEANS OF AN INTERMEDIARY NOTE

When ascending from a lower to a higher finger, glide with the last finger used, *i.e.* the lower finger; when descending, glide with the last finger used. Check intonation with open strings wherever possible. Repeat each section of the exercise several times.

SCALE OF D MAJOR
(G major, G minor and D minor can be practised with the same fingering.)

SCALE OF E MAJOR
(A major, A minor and E minor can be practised with the same fingering.)

* natural harmonic

STUDY IN FIRST AND THIRD POSITIONS

ADAM CARSE
Additional editing by Eta Cohen

Reproduced from Adam Carse, *New School of Violin Studies*. By permission of Stainer & Bell.

The intermediary 'shifting' notes should be played at first until their purpose is thoroughly understood. They should then be used silently.

A LITTLE PIECE

SCHUMANN

Gently ♩ = 138

STEP 21
ALLEGRETTO

MULLER

LARGO

HANDEL
arr. Ernest Haywood

N.B. 'Largo' in Handel's day meant a moderate, not a slow tempo.

STEP 22
MENUETT

DUSSEK
edited by Willy Burmester

STEP 23
MINUET IN G

BEETHOVEN

LONDONDERRY AIR

IRISH

STEP 24
AVE MARIA

J.S. BACH
arr. Gounod

THE LAST ROSE OF SUMMER

STEP 25
GAVOTTE IN D
(from *Orchestral Suite No. 3 in D*)

J.S. BACH

* 1st finger moves back a semitone but hand should remain in third position.

** Lower notes are original.

STEP 26
AVE MARIA

SCHUBERT
arr. Hermann Ries

* Double stopping optional.

STEP 27
SCALE OF E♭ MAJOR

MINUET
(from *Berenice*)

HANDEL

* Handel writes each time.

STEP 28
ENTR'ACTE
(from *Rosamunde*)

SCHUBERT

LA SERENATA

BRAGA

* Backward extension of 1st finger.

STEP 29
PRELUDIO, ALLEMANDA AND SARABANDA
(from *Sonata VIII*)
PRELUDIO

CORELLI

ALLEMANDA

SARABANDA

STEP 30
PRELUDIO AND TEMPO DI GAVOTTA
(from *Sonata IX*)
PRELUDIO

CORELLI

TEMPO DI GAVOTTA

ETA COHEN'S
VIOLIN METHOD

This highly respected violin course is the first choice for teachers in the UK and abroad. It includes the following material:

STARTING RIGHT

Covers the vital preliminaries to playing for the young beginner violinist, enlivened with colour illustrations. Includes accompaniment parts for violin duet and piano. (NOV916176)

BOOK 1

Student's Book (NOV916136) Violin part with teacher's notes. Divided into 30 Steps, each introducing a new technical point.
Accompaniment Book (NOV916137) Contains the piano accompaniments.
Teacher's Book (NOV916175) Violin duet parts and notes.
Learning to Play the Violin Three cassettes (NOV916167-01/02/03) and an instruction book (NOV916167) designed to accompany Book 1. The recordings provide the piano accompaniments and second violin parts.

BOOK 2

Student's Book (NOV916170) Every exercise and piece in this book is designed to improve and introduce new aspects of technique.
Accompaniment Book (NOV916171) Violin duet part and piano accompaniment.

BOOK 3

Student's Book (NOV916172) 30 graded lessons introducing technical points gradually, supported by numerous pieces.
Accompaniment Book (NOV916173) Contains the piano accompaniments.
Teacher's Book (NOV916174) Violin duet part.

BOOK 4

Complete Book (NOV916177) A wealth of valuable repertoire and studies which develop vital new areas of study. Includes violin part and piano accompaniments.

YOUNG RECITAL PIECES

Supplementary material for the Method books 1-4: three books of enjoyable pieces for young violinists, including many well-known works in easy arrangements. Each book contains the violin part and piano accompaniment.

> Book 1 (NOV916180)
> Book 2 (NOV916181)
> Book 3 (NOV916182)

EASY VIOLIN DUETS

Ideal for group teaching, introducing ensemble playing and making the early stages of learning more fun. These duets are carefully graded to be used alongside Starting Right and the Method books.

> Book 1 (NOV916184)
> Book 2 (NOV916185)
> Book 3 (NOV916186)

Novello Publishing Limited

Exclusive distributors:
Hal Leonard
7777 West Bluemound Road, Milwaukee, WI 53213
Email: info@halleonard.com
Hal Leonard Europe Limited
42 Wigmore Street Marylebone, London, WIU 2 RN
Email: info@halleonardeurope.com
Hal Leonard Australia Pty. Ltd.
4 Lentara Court Cheltenham, Victoria, 9132 Australia
Email: info@halleonard.com.au